KNOW
THE GAME

Gymnastics

Written in association with
British Gymnastics

BRITISH
GYMNASTICS

A&
CB

Produced for A & C Black by
Monkey Puzzle Media Ltd
Little Manor Farm, The Street
Brundish, Woodbridge
Suffolk IP13 8BL

Published in 2009 by

A & C Black Publishers Ltd
36 Soho Square, London W1D 3QY

Second edition 2009

Copyright © 2009, 1994
British Gymnastics

ISBN: 978 0 7136 8952 5

A CIP record for this book is available from the
British Library.

Note: While every effort has been made to ensure
that the content of this book is as technically accurate
and as sound as possible, neither the author nor the
publisher can accept responsibility for any injury or
loss sustained as a result of the use of this material.

This book is produced using paper that is made
from wood grown in managed, sustainable forests.
It is natural, renewable and recyclable. The logging
and manufacturing processes conform to the
environmental regulations of the country of origin.

Acknowledgements
Cover and inside design by James Winrow and
Tom Morris for Monkey Puzzle Media Ltd.
Cover photograph courtesy of Getty Images.
The publishers would like to thank the following for
permission to use photographs: Alan Edwards page
21; Getty Images pages 27, 30; Linda Gore pages 10,
11, 23, 25, 42, 44, 50; Rowena Humphrey page 47;
PA Photos pages 5, 54; Paul Seaby page 7.
All illustrations by © Adrian Stan.
The publishers would like to thank Brian Stocks, Jan
Charlton and Doreen Jones for their contributions to
this book.

KNOW THE GAME is a registered trademark.

Printed and bound in China by C&C Offset
Printing Co., Ltd.

CONTENTS

INTRODUCTION

At every Olympic Games, top gymnasts from around the world amaze audiences with their performances of athleticism and technical mastery. At international level, Russia, Romania and many of the former Eastern European nations have dominated the sport for many years, but the increasing success of the USA and China has started to balance out the field.

CLUBS AND SCHOOLS

As a direct result of its high profile at international events, gymnastics is now a popular sport that is practised widely in clubs and schools. This book has been written for the coach, the teacher, the gymnast and the spectator, to give a practical understanding of gymnastics at its most basic level. It will also give an insight into the preparation and skills that are essential to become a competitor in the sport.

DISCIPLINES

Gymnastics is divided into ten clearly defined disciplines.

1. Men's Artistic: men and boys compete on the floor, the pommel horse, rings, the vault, parallel bars and the high bar.

2. Women's Artistic: women and girls compete on the vault, asymmetric bars, the beam and the floor.

3. Rhythmic Gymnastics (women only): using hoop, ribbons, clubs, rope, ball and free exercise.

4. Trampoline: men's individual, women's individual and men's and women's synchronised.

5. Acrobatics: men's pairs, women's pairs, women's threes, mixed pairs and men's fours compete using their colleagues as the apparatus. This discipline also includes tumbling.

6. Gymnastics for All: includes pre-school, adult, display, festivals and trampette work.

7. Sports Aerobics: competitive form of aerobic movements performed to music. Competitors compete in groups and pairs as well as individually.

8. Team Gymnastics: Club Team competition involving six to twelve gymnasts, either men, women or mixed, competing in group floor exercises, streaming tumbling and streaming trampette and vault.

▶ Louis Smith of Great Britain celebrates his Bronze-winning performance on the pommel horse at the Beijing Olympics, 2008.

Gymnastics is one of the most popular Olympic spectator sports, with an even greater following than swimming.

9. Cheerleading: A new discipline of gymnastics adopted into the gymnastics family in 2008.

10. GMPD: The UK is the world leader in the inclusion of Gymnastics and Movement for People with Disabilities.

SAFETY

Gymnastics involves dynamic movement and rotation, so safety is especially vital. Safety precautions and good preparation should always be undertaken before starting any gymnastic activity. Coaches, teachers and gymnasts should carefully read the section n safety (see pages 10–11).

GOVERNING BODIES

- In Great Britain:
  British Gymnastics, Ford Hall, Lilleshall National Sports Centre, Newport, Shropshire TF10 9NB

  Tel: 0845 1297129
  Email:information@ british-gymnastics.org
  Website: www.british -gymnastics.org/

- Internationally:
  Gymnastics is governed by Fédération Internationale de Gymnastique (FIG), Rue des Oeuches 10, Case Postale 359, 2740 Moutier 1, Switzerland

  Email: webmaster@fig-gymnastics.org
  Website: www.fig-gymnastics.org/

EQUIPMENT AND CLOTHING

All apparatus should be of the proper specification and teachers should check it regularly to make sure that it has not become worn, damaged, tampered with or moved. Equipment used for competitions is normally approved by the Fédération Internationale de Gymnastique (FIG). All equipment must be annually maintained by an approved contractor.

APPARATUS

- School apparatus will usually include the following fundamental pieces: individual mats; small hand equipment; small apparatus; large apparatus; fixed apparatus.

- Where appropriate, the height of the adjustable apparatus should be altered so that it is suitable for junior performers.

- The layout of the apparatus should be carefully planned so the gymnasts do not hurt themselves when working on or dismounting from the equipment.

- Apparatus should not be too close to doors, windows and radiators.

- Apparatus should be laid out with sufficient space between pieces.

- Never use apparatus that you do not feel confident working with.

- Apparatus must never be used without a responsible qualified adult or qualified coach in attendance.

▼ A well-spaced, safe gymnasium layout.

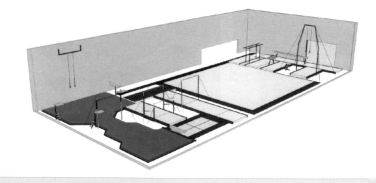

- Employ a qualified company to check and maintain school gymnasium equipment at least once a year and keep a copy of the written report. Your local authority or national governing body will be able to advise on recognised companies that can be contracted to do this work.

- Never use a piece of equipment that is faulty or has been condemned, even if it looks sound and in working order.

CLOTHING

- Clothing should be close-fitting so it will not catch on the apparatus. Loose, baggy clothes should be removed or tucked in.

- Socks should not be worn without suitable shoes.

- Long hair should be tied back.

- Jewellery or body piercing adornments must be removed by coaches and participants.

- The teacher's own footwear, jewellery and hair should conform to safety standards.

COMPETITION CLOTHING

The FIG's Code of Points has the following rules for competition clothing.

Men

- On the pommel horse, rings, parallel bars and horizontal bar: competitors must wear long, solid-coloured competition pants and footwear (gymnastics slippers or socks).

- On the floor and vault: gymnasts may wear short pants and perform without footwear.

- The wearing of a competition jersey is mandatory in all competitions.

Women

- Leotards can be short or long-sleeved, with wide shoulder straps.

- The leg cut of the leotard may not extend beyond the hip bone.

- Slippers and socks are optional.

A range of suitable clothing.

COMPETITION AND TRAINING

In competitions, gymnasts build sequences (routines) of exercises on selected pieces of apparatus or the floor and perform them in front of a panel of judges.

EVENTS

In artistic gymnastic events, women compete on the floor, vault, asymmetric bars (uneven parallel bars) and beam. Men compete on the floor, pommel horse, rings, vault, parallel bars and high bar.

ROUTINES

Routines are either compulsory or voluntary at beginner level. At international, world and Olympic level, routines are now only voluntary but do have to contain some compulsory elements.

In compulsory routines, the sequence of movements is pre-designed and all gymnasts must attempt to perform the same skills in the same way.

In voluntary routines, gymnasts are free to include their own elements, and they may choose to select difficult elements to raise their difficulty score. Of course, they must be able to perform them well so that the judges do not deduct too many marks for poor execution. Normally, the level of difficulty required as a minimum is laid down in the competition rules, and voluntary routines should match or exceed that level of difficulty to avoid deductions for being short on content. Difficulty scores are now open-ended, with score levels being set only by the skill of the gymnast.

TRAINING

Gymnasts need many qualities to be top-class performers, including discipline, strength, endurance, flexibility and spatial awareness. Many gymnasts are born with ability in one or several of these areas, but to learn the whole range of skills involved requires considerable dedication and training.

A top-class gymnast will train six or seven days a week for two or three sessions each day. Each training session can last several hours. Learning the basic skills can easily be achieved in one or two sessions a week, but as the skills become more difficult, the amount of time spent training has to be increased.

JUDGING

At international, world and Olympic competitions there are now two panels of judges – an A and B panel. The A panel (two judges) assesses the difficulty, which is open-ended and is a summation of the difficulty performed in a routine. The B panel (six judges) deducts the technical errors from a starting score of 10.00. The highest and lowest individual judges' scores are ignored and the average of the remaining four is then calculated. The two scores (A and B) are then added together to produce the final score. This score will often be in excess of 16.00. These new scoring levels are open-ended and will increase with perfection in execution and increased difficulty.

At regional and club competition level four judges may be used on the B panel. In this case the average of the middle two scores in the range is used to obtain the average score.

COACHING

All gymnastic activity should take place in the presence of a qualified coach or teacher. A coach is responsible for the safety and care of gymnasts under his or her control.

When you first start gymnastics, you will normally just compete on the floor and vault.

Judging a vault.

Judge's scoring keypad.

SAFETY IN THE GYMNASIUM

Gymnastics is not a dangerous sport as long as it is properly planned and care is taken. Injuries normally occur through negligence or lack of planning. To ensure a completely safe environment, the following aspects need to be considered: the layout of equipment, learning of new skills, gymnast safety, and the level of qualification of the teacher/coach.

LAYOUT OF EQUIPMENT

- Make sure that apparatus is safe before it is used. It must be firmly anchored to the ground where appropriate, with all cables, guy ropes and fixings sufficiently tightened to minimise excessive movement.

- Apparatus should be well-spaced so that there is enough room for gymnasts to mount and dismount, and in case of a fall.

- If the apparatus is not mounted over a foam safety pit, sufficient mats must be arranged beneath and around it. Ensure there are no gaps between the mats. Use large safety mattresses 30cm thick to make the area even safer.

- The gymnasium hall should be clean. Floor surfaces should not be slippery, especially if children are working in bare feet.

- Apparatus should be stored safely and neatly. It is better to store apparatus around the hall than in one area, as children can access it more easily if necessary.

A young gymnast practises balancing on mats, with a coach spotting.

LEARNING NEW SKILLS

- Training should only take place in the presence of a qualified coach or teacher. The coach or teacher must be in attendance at all times.

- Gymnasts must warm up thoroughly before starting more strenuous training, and difficult skills should be introduced slowly, or broken into key component parts, so as not to tax the gymnast too far.

- Gymnasts should never be allowed to work beyond their level of ability.

- If the coach is concerned about the safety of the gymnast, additional matting should be placed around the apparatus to cushion a fall. In situations involving inversion, always use a safety mattress approximately 30cm thick.

- The coach should consider the size of the group and the level of control that he/she can offer, especially when teaching children. It may be necessary to progress at a slower rate with a larger group. The gymnasts' safety should be ensured at all times.

GYMNAST SAFETY

- Gymnasts should be properly dressed.

- Gymnasts should be thoroughly warmed up.

- Gymnasts should be trained and conditioned in parts of a new skill before attempting the whole element.

A coach is present during the jump phase of the sequence.

THE WARM-UP

A correct warm-up and body preparation is essential to any training programme. It should prepare the body and lay the foundations for the strenuous work that is to follow. It will also have a positive mental effect, so gymnasts feel better and more ready for work. The gymnast and coach must warm up at the beginning of every practice session, however short.

WARM-UP ACTIVITIES

The warm-up should consist of running and jogging activities that raise the overall body temperature and prepare the cardiovascular system. These should be closely followed by stretching and limbering exercises to stretch and prepare the muscles, associated ligaments and connective tissues for the forthcoming work, and contain work that will relate to the main activity. Finally, it should prepare the neuromuscular system and contain mobility exercises to prepare the joints. The minimum warm-up duration should be 5–10 minutes for a lesson of 25–30 minutes.

VALUE OF THE WARM-UP

- Prepares the body for exercise.
- Helps to prevent injury.
- Helps to improve motivation.

TYPICAL WARM-UP

A typical warm-up begins with general jogging, running and skipping around the gymnasium until the gymnasts feel warm. Exercises that use the majority of the muscles should be included, such as arm and leg swinging, and trunk circling. Games such as tag chin, leap frog and catch are also good motivators for young gymnasts.

A warm-up should incorporate running, dance and jogging activities, stretching and limbering, and basic body conditioning.

A range of suppling exercises designed to mobilise and exercise the major joints fully and safely.

Once they begin to feel warm, the gymnasts should progress to more specific supling exercises (see above), which mobilise and exercise all the major joints, such as the wrists, elbows, shoulders, neck, back, hips, knees and ankles.

FLEXIBILITY OR SUPPLING

When the joints have been sufficiently manipulated, gymnasts can increase their range of movement by doing a range of supling activities. A good level of flexibility is essential because it helps the gymnast to assume the correct body position and minimises injury if the muscles are accidentally over-stretched.

Some basic movements will be difficult for children and gymnasts who have not achieved sufficient suppleness within the joints.

Many children are unable to place their hands fully above their heads or even to sit on the floor with their backs at 90° to the ground.

BODY SYSTEMS

The warm-up must prepare all the body systems:

- cardiovascular, cardiorespiratory: heart, lungs, blood vessels

- muscular-skeletal: bones, muscles, tendons, ligaments, connective tissue

- neuromuscular: circulation, body, brain.

JUMPING

Jumps are made up of many different movements, including landings, and are best performed and learnt on the floor or from a box. In any jump, it is important to land with the knees bent and feet slightly apart in the 'plié' position (feet angled at 45°) to protect the knee joints.

STANDING UPWARD JUMP

- Bending your legs slightly, jump up while raising your arms forwards and upwards above your head. Keep your arms slightly in front of your body.

- As you land, it is important to keep your arms raised above your head, and place your feet slightly apart in the 'plié' position at an angle of 45°, with your knees bent. As you make contact with the floor continue to bend the knees to absorb the downward force of landing. Bring your arms down sideways to stabilise the landing, without taking a step.

Standing upward jump with full turn.

TEACHING TIP

If the arms are thrown too vigorously upwards there will be a tendency for the gymnast's shoulders to move backwards.

STANDING UPWARD JUMP WITH FULL TURN

- Begin the upward jump as described above.

- To initiate the full turn, push strongly with your feet in the direction of the turn and raise your arms more forcefully up and across your body to assist the spin.

- Keep the body fully stretched throughout this movement to allow the full turn to proceed more easily.

- Try to 'spot' a landing place before taking off. If you look for that place before you land it will assist the landing phase. This technique is known as 'spotting'.

- Bring your arms down to the side to slow the spin down and help with the landing. Try not to step to control the landing.

> **TEACHING TIP**
>
> Make sure that gymnasts try this jump on soft mats, so they can land safely if they lose their balance. Young children find this skill particularly difficult due to their relatively large heads.

ASTRIDE JUMP FROM BOX

- As you leave the box top, spread your legs and arms out so that your body forms a star shape in the air.
- On approaching the floor, quickly bring your legs together and attempt to land still, with your knees slightly bent, without any extra movement of the feet. Extend your arms and legs to full stretch to finish the move and show the judges you are in full control.

Astride jump from box.

TUCKED JUMP FROM BOX

- Bend your legs and swing your arms down to your knees.
- Quickly straighten your legs and at the same time, swing your arms upwards and forwards.
- At the height of the jump, quickly bend your legs and bring your knees up to your chest, then just as quickly stretch out again in preparation for the landing.

Tucked jump from box.

> **TEACHING TIP**
>
> The coach should stand to one side of the gymnast and take hold of their chest to make sure the performer does not over-rotate.

VAULTING

The vault is one of the first pieces of apparatus that should be introduced to the beginner gymnast. Vaulting is an exciting and exhilarating activity, suitable for all ages as long as the height of the vault has been suitably adjusted.

PHASES OF THE VAULT

The vault is divided into seven distinct phases:

1. approach run

2. hurdle step

3. take-off

4. pre-flight

5. strike

6. post-flight

7. landing.

 The seven phases of the vault.

Every vault requires these phases to come together in harmony. A good vault consists of an aggressive approach, followed by a very powerful flight and strike movement. The gymnast is attempting to transfer as much power as possible from the run-up to the components of height and rotation.

The gymnast and coach should spend the initial learning period mastering the approach run and take-off from the springboard. It is important to have a consistent run-up and to be able to take off from the springiest part of the board every time.

TYPES OF VAULT

There are two types of vault (see diagrams below and top of page 17):

1. Horizontal: the heels rise on take-off and return to the floor after the strike phase.

2. Vertical: the heels continue to rise after the strike phase and pass over the head to the floor.

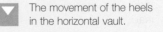 The movement of the heels in the horizontal vault.

The movement of the heels in a vertical vault.

SQUAT ON TO AND JUMP OFF BOX WITH STRAIGHT BODY

- From a short run and hurdle step (in which the feet are hopped together), land with two feet in front of the box.

- Place your hands on the box top and, jumping hard from the floor, raise your hips and squat your feet close to your hands.

- In order to raise the hips sufficiently it is important to press strongly against the box top. Allow the shoulders to move forwards slightly over the hands as the hips are raised.

- Jumping off the box, quickly straighten your legs and stretch your body, placing your arms over your head.

- Keeping your head up in the jump, quickly focus your attention to the spot on the floor where you are going to land.

- On landing, bend at the ankles, knees and hips to absorb the energy from the jump.

TEACHING TIP

It may be necessary to help very young gymnasts in one of the phases. In the take-off phase, support can be given from the side by taking hold of the gymnast's near shoulder and stomach. In the post-flight phase, the coach should stand either to one side or in front and take hold of the gymnast's chest, controlling the rotation so the gymnast achieves a safe and steady landing.

Squat on to and jump off the box with a straight body.

Straddle vault over box.

STRADDLE VAULT OVER BUCK OR CROSS-BOX

- From a short approach, run and hurdle step.

- Jump upwards and forwards, quickly placing your hands on the box top. Push strongly.

- As the hips rise, straddle your legs and allow your shoulders to move slightly forwards over your hands.

- As you strike the box top with your hands, your body will begin to rise.

- Once in flight, bring your feet together whilst at the same time quickly stretching your body.

- Concentrate on keeping your chest up and preparing for the landing.

TEACHING TIP

You can help beginners to straddle on to the box top by standing in front of them and supporting their chest close to the top of their arms. Keep your head to one side. At the appropriate moment and with several practices, you can help the gymnast over the box. Beginners who do not straddle their legs sufficiently often catch their feet on the box, so either support the gymnast or place a soft safety mat on the other side of the vault.

A strong push will carry the gymnast over the box and return their feet to the ground. Beginners have a tendency not to push strongly enough.

HEADSPRING OVER CROSS-BOX

- Approach this vault with a short run and a hurdle step on to the springboard.
- Place your hands centrally on the box and jump, raising your hips well above your shoulders.
- As the hips rise, bend your arms and place your head lightly on the box top. Your body will be bent at the hips.
- As your hips pass over your hands and head, push strongly with your arms, at the same time extending the hips and driving your heels upwards and forwards in the direction of flight.
- Arch your body and continue to push against the box top until your arms are fully extended.
- Maintain this extended body position until your feet contact the floor.
- On landing bend your legs and keep your head up.

TEACHING TIP

The cross-box can be lowered to help the first part of the movement, especially if the gymnasts are very young. Be aware that the lower the box, the easier the first flight and more difficult the second flight. The higher the box, the more difficult the first flight and easier the second flight. You could make the approach side of the box lower by placing two benches side by side for the gymnasts to work off. Place suitable matting in the landing area because gymnasts can land with an arched back when learning this skill.

Headspring vault.

HANDSPRING

This vertical vault has sometimes been referred to as a 'longarm vault', but the modern term for it is now handspring. It is one of the hardest skills by far to perform correctly because the body has to be raised a considerable height above the ground and with sufficient rotation to be able to regain the standing position.

- To obtain the necessary height and rotation, a fast but controlled approach run is required.

- On take-off, drive your arms upwards and extend the body.

- Think of the lower body rotating over the upper body.

- You must still be moving upwards at the point when your hands strike the vault.

- In the strike phase, the angle of the body and the vault should be between 60 and 80 degrees to the vertical.

- Your hands should leave the box just before your body reaches the vertical. To achieve this the strike phase must be short and extremely powerful.

- During post-flight, keep the body as straight as possible.

- Just before landing, bend the knees.

TEACHING TIP

The handspring requires tremendous coordination of speed and power. Beginners find it particularly difficult to raise the body to the required position without losing rotation and power. Be prepared for a poor second flight and stand on the landing side of the vault, supporting the gymnast's upper back to assist the rotation back to the feet. If the gymnast is unable to complete a strong strike phase, grasp the wrist with your second hand as the gymnast strikes the box. This will prevent the gymnast from over-rotating. If you reach over the box, you will be able to give a little lift to any gymnast needing more rotation.

 Handspring vault.

Nicola Willis of Great Britain performs in the Women's Vault at the 2004 Olympic Games in Athens.

THE FAMILY OF ROLLS

Rolling is the most basic and fundamental skill in gymnastics. It is important that great care is taken to master the technique correctly, as many of the basic shapes and controls that are used in the more complex skills are developed at this early stage.

BASIC POSITION FOR THE FAMILY OF ROLLS

- Lying flat on your back, draw your knees up to your chest. Curl up tight to make a rounded back, then rock backwards and forwards, holding your knees tightly.

- Rock backwards and forwards with a little more power. When your feet make contact with the ground, stretch forwards with your arms and attempt to stand.

- From standing, crouch down, roll back on to your shoulders and rock back to your feet.

The basic position.

FORWARD ROLL

- From standing, crouch down. Place your hands on the floor in front of you, shoulder-width apart with your fingers facing forwards, while simultaneously placing your chin on your chest. This will ensure that your hips are raised high enough and your spine is rounded so that you can roll on to your back.

- Bend your arms as you place your neck on the floor, slightly extending the legs and pushing on the floor with your feet until the roll commences and you roll on to your back.

- Try to keep your legs straight as you commence the roll forwards. In the very last part of the roll, bend your legs tightly so that your heels are close to your bottom.

- At the point where your feet make contact with the floor, stretch forwards with your arms so that your head and chest move over your feet. Once your body weight is in a position of balance you will be able to stand.

Forward roll.

Coaches help a young gymnast master the basics of forward roll.

TEACHING TIPS

- Beginners will find it tempting to use their hands to help them stand. This should be avoided at all costs.

- You can help in the final phase of this movement by standing in front of the gymnast and taking hold of their arms to help them get to their feet.

BACKWARD ROLL

- From standing, lower to a squat position with your back well rounded.

- Allow your body to move backwards so that your body weight falls back over your heels until your bottom makes contact with the floor.

- Roll your body backwards until your shoulders make contact with the ground. As this happens, move your hands quickly to a position just above your shoulders, with your fingers facing upwards and your palms down, elbows held high. Your fingertips should make contact with the ground, then your palms.

- As the rolling movement takes place, put your chin on your chest and press with your hands so that as little weight as possible is put on your head.

- When your shoulders make contact with the floor, push against it strongly with your hands by straightening your arms. This raises the hips slightly and takes the weight off the head.

- Continue to rotate your body, still maintaining the curled position, until your feet reach the ground. The movement is finished in a squat or standing position.

TEACHING TIPS

- You can support the backward roll by taking hold of the gymnast's waist at the point at which they roll on to their shoulders. You can then gently lift the gymnast's hips over their head to aid the actual rolling movement, whilst at the same time reducing the amount of weight felt by their head.

- As the head of most junior gymnasts is relatively large in comparison to the rest of their body, many find this movement quite difficult. They will tend to twist and turn the head and roll over one shoulder. This is an acceptable way of rolling, but they should be taught very quickly how to roll while using their hands to support their body weight, so that the turning of the head does not become a difficult habit to break.

Backward roll.

TUCKED SIDEWAYS ROLL

- Starting in a kneeling position, arms outstretched to the sides, allow yourself to sink back on to your heels and fall to the side.
- Keep your knees close to your chest as you roll over on to your back and return to the hands-and-knees starting position.

TEACHING TIP

By standing over the gymnast, you can assist and guide the correct alignment of the roll and for the final phase, help the gymnast back to their feet.

 Tucked sideways roll.

Children of all ages can get involved in gymnastics.

SIDEWAYS ROLL

- Start with one leg stretched and one knee bent.

- Lower your body forwards while simultaneously tipping sideways. Roll on to your back. Bend the outstretched leg to allow the body to roll across the back.

- At the point at which the alternate knee makes contact with the floor, stretch the opposite leg to arrive back in a mirror image position of the one in which you started.

Sideways roll.

LONG SIDEWAYS ROLL (LOG ROLL)

- Lying flat on the floor, with your arms and legs outstretched, lift your hands and feet slightly. Move both your arms and your legs to one side.

- As your weight is transferred and your body tips on to its side, you will begin to roll.

- Draw your arms and legs back into a straight line position with the rest of your body, arms above your head, feet stretched below your body.

- As your body continues to roll, bring your arms back behind your head while hollowing and extending your legs backwards.

- You will now roll on to your stomach.

- By continuing to stretch your arms and legs in the direction of the roll, you will now roll from your stomach on to your side.

- At this point you can bring your arms and legs forwards slightly, allowing yourself to roll on to your back.

Log roll.

TEACHING TIP

Most beginners will be able to do this roll with their arms and legs on the floor, so even the less-able child will be able to complete rolling using this technique.

▶ Louis Smith competes in the individual men's pommel horse final in the Beijing 2008 Olympics. He won the Bronze medal.

TIN SOLDIER ROLL (CIRCLE ROLL)

- Sit on the floor, legs in straddle.
- Take hold of your legs just below the knees.
- With a slight dynamic movement of the body to the left or the right, topple over on to your shoulder.
- By folding more tightly towards the legs you can roll across the middle of your back and return to the original sitting position.
- As this movement requires no change in position once the overbalancing has been achieved, you can retain a fairly rigid body shape without moving to complete the roll.

TEACHING TIP

You may need to stand behind the gymnast to help them roll on the correct part of the shoulders – from the middle of the back to the shoulder blades. Many beginners do not roll high enough across the shoulders and therefore find this movement quite difficult.

ROLL VARIATIONS

Once you have mastered the basic family of rolls, you can start to try different variations. The first two variations below are ideal for beginners or very young children. The rest are for more advanced gymnasts.

ROLLING WITH A PLATFORM

Many beginners have difficulty standing up at the finish of a forward roll. Sitting on the end of a platform, rock backwards and forwards and then stand.

▲ Rolling with a platform.

ROLLING FROM A BOX TOP

- Using two or three sections of a box and an additional landing mat, lie on the box on your stomach.

- Move forwards so that your hands and chest are hanging over the end of the box and can be placed on the mat on the ground.

- Slowly adjusting the amount of weight that is resting on the box top and transferring it to your hands, tuck your chin to your chest and lower your body on to your upper shoulders.

- Then, by curling your body, start a forwards roll.

 Rolling from a box top.

FORWARD ROLL WITH STRAIGHT LEGS TO STRADDLE

- While rolling over your back in a forward roll your legs must be kept straight.

- As you approach the lower part of your back in the roll, straddle your legs wide.

The wider the straddle, the easier the movement is to perform.

Method 1

- As soon as your heels touch the floor, place your hands on the floor (between your legs and close to the crotch). Push hard with your hands and lean well forwards. Try to get your head and chest in front of your feet.

- Continue to press against the floor for as long as possible until your fingers leave the floor.

- Continue to bend your body forwards until your body weight is completely over your feet. You will then be able to stretch out in the straddle stand position and raise your body.

Method 2 (slightly harder)

By following this method you can stand without using your hands on the floor.

- As your heels make contact with the floor, press them down on the ground.

- Reach forwards with your arms and chest so that your bottom rises from the ground to a position of balance in line with your feet.

- Control the balance position and stop the forward movement of the body by moving your arms backwards into a position of balance.

Method 2: Forward roll with straight legs to straddle.

29

BACKWARD ROLL TO STRIDE STAND

- Start the movement in the same way as the backward roll, rolling over on to your back.

- As you roll on to your shoulders and neck, begin to straighten your legs.

- As soon as your hands are placed firmly on the floor, push strongly against the floor to raise your hips over your head.

- When your hips are directly over your hands, straddle your legs and lower your feet to the floor, close to your hands.

- To finish in a stride stand, push vigorously with both hands. Then raise your head and chest to a position of balance.

TEACHING TIP

You can help the gymnast in the final phase of movement by supporting their hips when they reach their highest point. This will remove some of the weight from the gymnast's hands and help as the feet are lowered to the floor.

Backward roll to astride.

The England team (left to right: Luke Folwell, Ryan Bradley, Ross Brewer, Louis Smith and Kristian Thomas) celebrates winning the Bronze medal in the Men's Team competition, Melbourne 2006 Commonwealth Games.

BACKWARD ROLL PASSING THROUGH HANDSTAND

This is a natural extension of the backward roll to stride stand. It can be learnt progressively by practising the basic backward roll, concentrating on pushing the hips to the ceiling and simultaneously stretching out the legs.

- Perform the first part of the roll in exactly the same way as for the backward roll to stride stand.

- With this movement it is important to move the hands to the shoulders as quickly as possible.

- As soon as your hands make contact with the floor, ensure that they are in a position just above the shoulders, with the fingers facing the body and the elbows held high.

- Push strongly with both hands and arms, at the same time extending the hips and legs (straighten the body) towards the ceiling.

- Timing is the key to this movement because the extension to the ceiling and the arm push should happen simultaneously and at such a rate that the body is vertically extended.

TEACHING TIP

You can help the gymnast by taking hold of the feet as the hands contact the floor. You can then lift the gymnast through the movement, drawing the feet to a position above the hands into a straight handstand.

For this movement to be performed correctly, the body should momentarily pass through a held handstand position.

 Backward roll passing through handstand.

31

WEIGHT ON HANDS

Movements that involve the transfer of weight from the feet to the hands include the bridge, cartwheel and round-off (Arabian spring). They require sufficient strength in the shoulders and spine to support the full weight of the gymnast.

BRIDGE

- Start by lying on your back.

- Draw your knees up so that your feet are close to your bottom.

- Stretch your arms above your head, bending them so that your elbows are raised towards the ceiling and your hands are placed on the floor, with the fingers pointing back to your shoulders.

- Your hands should be close to your head (be careful not to trap any long hair).

- From this position, push against the floor with your hands and feet so that your bottom and back are raised from the floor to arrive in the bridge.

- The movement is complete when both arms and legs are completely straight. Make sure that your ankles and knees are pressed tightly together.

> In the ideal bridge position, the shoulders lie directly over, or slightly in front of, the hands.

TEACHING TIP

Beginners will need help at first because the bridge is not easy until the shoulders and spine have developed enough flexibility, along with sufficient strength to support the full weight of the gymnast. You can give support by lifting the gymnast under the shoulders as the bridge position is adopted.

Bridge.

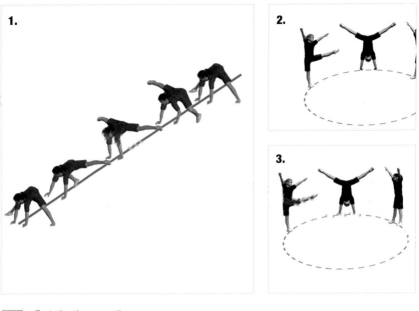

Cartwheel preparation
1, 2 and 3.

CARTWHEEL

The key to success in this movement is the ability to be able to do both a handstand and a side handstand with legs straddled.

Preparation for the cartwheel

1. Standing on all fours straddling a line, jump from one leg to the other over the line.

2. Stand on one side of a line. Place one hand on one side of the line. Simultaneously jumping your legs over the supporting hand, place the second hand over the line and allow the feet to drop to the ground.

3. Draw a circle on the ground. Stand on the circle and place the first foot, the first hand, the second hand and the second foot on the points around the circle while the eyes look at the centre of the circle.

COACHING NOTE

The gymnast should be encouraged to get the hips and shoulders directly over the hands.

SINGLE CARTWHEEL

At the start of this movement you can either face the direction in which you intend to go, or stand sideways. The method described here is the former. The whole sequence should be completed in a straight line.

- Raise your hands above your head and place your leading leg forward.

- Reach forward to place the first hand (the hand on the same side as the leading leg) on the floor by bending your front leg and also bending at the waist.

- When the first hand makes contact with the floor, straighten your front leg while kicking upwards with your back leg over your head.

- Continue the movement by rocking over from your first to your second hand (which is still extended above your head). To do this, push strongly against the floor with your first hand, keeping your arms stretched up over your head.

- As your body rocks over your second hand, bring your second leg down to the ground and place it close to your second hand.

TEACHING TIPS

- Emphasise the point of pushing strongly with the second hand to arrive in a stretched standing position.

- Stand behind the gymnast, and if the left leg leads the cartwheel, place your right hand on the left hip. You will then be able to help the overall rotation and the final phase of arriving back on the feet.

Starting with your left leg, the sequence of movement is: left foot, left hand, right hand, right foot.

Single cartwheel with support.

Two cartwheels.

TWO CARTWHEELS

In this movement, two cartwheels are performed, one after the other, exactly as described opposite. However, the second cartwheel will always be done from a sideways-facing position.

- In the first cartwheel, remember to push hard with the second hand as it makes contact with the floor. This will increase the speed of the movement for the second cartwheel and allow it to proceed smoothly from the first.

- Bend your legs slightly as your feet come into contact with the floor. Your feet should be turned out to facilitate the necessary control coming into the first landing and the push going into the second cartwheel.

TEACHING TIPS

- If the legs are kept perfectly straight there will be a tendency to hesitate before moving into the second cartwheel.

- The gymnast should concentrate hard on moving down a straight line.

- When this skill is performed correctly the gymnast will have no problems in doing a series of continuous cartwheels. When performing a series it does look very much like a coach wheel rolling down a mat.

ROUND-OFF (ARABIAN SPRING)

This movement is basically a cartwheel with a quarter-turn during the hand placement phase. In a cartwheel, both hands and feet move along a straight line, but in a round-off, the second hand is placed slightly out of alignment with the first.

- Starting with a small run and a skip-step, stretch the arms overhead. If you are leading with the left, the skip-step consists of the following ground contact: right foot, right foot, left foot, hand placement.

- Lean well forwards. Bend the leading leg and bend at the waist to place your left hand on the floor.

- Immediately and quickly straighten your left leg, while at the same time swinging your right leg upwards into a cartwheel action.

- Your body will simultaneously twist around the left hand so as to place the right hand out of alignment with the left.

- As soon as both hands are in contact with the floor the legs, which are trailing behind in the direction of travel, are snapped down to the ground. Push hard with your hands at the same time (this is all happening while the quarter-turn is completed).

- In a good round-off, you should land facing the direction from which you have come, with your feet either side of an imaginary line. In this way the forward movement is transferred into backward movement.

- Land with your arms raised above your head and your body in a semi-crouched position.

The round-off is a key movement in gymnastics, turning forward movement very efficiently into backward movement.

Round-off (Arabian spring).

TEACHING TIPS

The round-off is best done in stages:

1. Perform a cartwheel with a quarter-turn, bringing the second leg to meet the first.

2. Repeat the movement several times, each time reducing the time the second leg takes to join the first.

3. Eventually, bring both feet together in flight simultaneously to land with feet together.

4. Finally, perform the round-off from a couple of running steps with the emphasis on bouncing out of the landing.

Preparation 1
Performing a round-off from a springboard will help the gymnast push out of the movement and encourage the necessary flight from the hands.

 Round-off preparation 1.

Preparation 2
Performing the round-off over a rolled-up mat will encourage the gymnast to get the essential flight using a strong push from the hands.

Round-off preparation 2.

BALANCING

Balancing movements include the arabesque, headstand and handstands. They all require a certain level of flexibility and a feel for the balance position.

ARABESQUE

This movement relies heavily on the gymnast's flexibility or range of movement.

- Start by standing on one leg, with the other leg stretched behind you, the top of your big toe resting on the floor.

- Raise the free leg upwards behind you, keeping your back straight.

- Fix your gaze on a point in front of you to help you maintain your balance.

- Continue to raise your leg to the full extent of your suppleness.

- As you raise your leg, continue to lower your chest. Keep your head up to allow your back to hollow.

- Lift your arms either forwards or to the side, following the line made by the raised leg, so that an aesthetic pose is achieved.

TEACHING TIPS

- Actively encourage improvement in flexibility, working on it during the warm-up.

- The necessary angles in the shoulder may not be possible for the gymnast to achieve if they do not have the required flexibility.

BRIDGE

The bridge (as described on page 32) is also a movement that can be performed under a 'balancing' theme.

Arabesque with different arm positions.

HEADSTAND FROM CROUCH POSITION

- Crouch down and place your hands and forehead on the floor to form an equilateral triangle (see diagram). Your head should be approximately 30cm in front of your hands and your arms bent at an angle of 90 degrees.

- Extend your legs so that your pointed toes are resting on the floor.

- By pressing with your hands, slowly move your bottom over your forehead into a balanced position. Maintain the equilibrium by continually pressing with your hands.

- By exerting more pressure you will reach a point at which you can lift your feet from the floor.

- Continue to raise your legs above your head by pressing constantly against the floor with your hands. Make sure that your back is kept straight at all times by tightening your bottom and stomach muscles.

- As your legs move above your shoulders you will need to draw your bottom back slightly to prevent yourself from toppling over.

- To maintain balance it should feel as though your body is 'wishing' to return to the ground, and that this is only being prevented by the contact pressure exerted through the hands.

TEACHING TIP

Help gymnasts by taking hold of their hips and making sure that they adopt the correct position as they find their balance.

In a headstand (left), the pattern drawn by your head and hands should be an equilateral triangle.

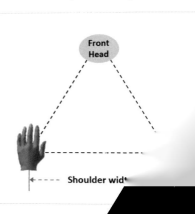

Front Head

Shoulder wid*

HEADSTAND WITH KNEES BENT

- Start from crouch.
- Place your hands and forehead on the floor to form a triangle (see page 39), with your head approximately 30cm in front of your hands.
- Your arms should be bent at 90 degrees, elbows pointing to the ceiling.
- Slowly move your feet in closer to your hands until your hips lie above the triangle base.
- Push down strongly with your hands on the floor. As your feet leave the floor, feel for the balance position.
- Your knees should be bent tightly with your back held straight. This straight-backed position allows your weight to be evenly distributed over your hands and head.

TEACHING TIP

Encourage the gymnast to maintain a straight-backed position. Beginners tend to hollow their back, which places excessive pressure on their head and neck.

Headstand with knees bent.

HANDSTAND WITH SUPPORT

The handstand is one of the key basic positions in gymnastics and it is required in the development of many other skills. Initially, the handstand should not be attempted without support. The role of the supporter is described in the teaching tips box opposite.

- Start from a standing position with your arms raised over your head, shoulder-width apart.

- Take a long step forwards, bending the front leg. Place both hands on the floor approximately shoulder-width apart, fingers facing forwards.

- Straighten the front leg while at the same time kicking and thrusting the back leg into a position above your shoulders.

- As the driving leg nears the position of balance, bring your other leg to join it so that both legs arrive simultaneously in the handstand position.

The gymnast must do most of the work and must not be over-supported.

- The shoulders must first move forwards over the hands, returning to a position directly above the hands once the handstand position has been achieved. This creates the feeling of balance.

- Constant pressure is maintained through the fingers to maintain balance.

- The handstand itself must be absolutely straight: if a straight line was drawn from the hands to the feet, it should pass straight through the middle of the body.

- The supporter must stand facing the gymnast, who places their hands on the ground just in front of one of the supporter's feet. The supporter then grabs the gymnast by the hips, assisting their arrival in the balance position. Once in the balance position, the supporter should only 'feather support' the gymnast so that they are able to control the skill themselves.

- Make sure that the gymnast is in a vertical position, thus learning how to balance on the hands.

Handstand with support.

HANDSTAND

The handstand held freely is a natural progression from the handstand with support (see page 41).

- Make sure that your body is held quite straight, with the emphasis upon complete extension of the shoulders and a straight-line relationship between arms, body and legs.

- Point your toes towards the ceiling.

- Avoid letting your body weight simply rest on the hands; concentrate on pressing the body up as far as possible.

◀ A gymnast performs a handstand hold freely.

TEACHING TIPS

- There must be constant pressure between the heel of the hand and the fingertips.

- Since the relative strength of the arms is far less when supporting the body in handstand, the balance position is critical and will take some time for the beginner to learn.

Practice against a wall

One way to learn the handstand is to balance against a wall. Note that before attempting this, gymnasts must be able to support their body weight on straight arms, and demonstrate this to a supporter.

- Place your hands approximately 20–30cm from the wall and kick to handstand (see page 41).

- You must be able to kick to handstand and return to the floor by pressing against the wall with the heels, without collapsing.

- Once you have mastered this confidently, move your hands closer and closer to the wall until your fingers are about 12.5cm away. You will then be forced into achieving a straight handstand, because if the body is bent in any way you will fall back down to the ground.

- Once you are successfully able to kick to a handstand with your fingers almost touching the wall, you must learn to tense the muscles in your body, especially in your bottom, so that it is under constant tension and as straight and as stiff as possible.

- Then, by applying constant force through the fingertips, you will find that your heels will drift slightly from the wall. By constantly applying and releasing this pressure you will be able to remain in this position with your feet very close to the wall but not actually touching it. It is particularly important that you 'feel' the overbalance position.

(see page 41)

TEACHING TIPS

- The more flexible a performer, the less force is required to kick into the handstand position and therefore less force has to be caught and balanced on the hands. It is very important to work on flexibility so the gymnast can achieve the correct position with the minimum of force.

- Eventually, encourage the gymnast to start practicing the handstand in the middle of the gym floor, learning to kick into a held position. The movement will have been thoroughly learnt when the gymnast can arrive in handstand without bending the arms or 'walking' the hands to regain balance.

Handstand against a wall.

Recovery from the handstand

When gymnasts first attempt the handstand in the middle of the floor, they often overbalance. They should be taught how to turn out of the movement, and sufficient matting must be placed on the ground so they can roll out of it if necessary.

Sustaining the handstand

The next skill is to kick to handstand and hold the balance perfectly still for 3 seconds or more. A lot of practice is required if the gymnast is to deliver the right amount of force to arrive in the handstand, and to continue to apply the pressure through the fingers without overbalancing.

Equilibrium

When attempting the handstand, the gymnast aims to achieve a state of equilibrium in which the heel of the hand is the balance point for the body, which is maintained by applying a constant force through the fingers. Many beginner gymnasts throw themselves into a position on their hands without understanding the role played by their fingers and arms in maintaining the handstand. The coach must emphasise the importance of this role.

A gymnast can recover from overbalancing in a handstand by rolling out of it.

HANDSTAND ON BENCH

Once the handstand has been mastered on the floor it can be attempted on a bench. This is a good preparation for transferring the movement to the beam.

- Place your hands on the outside edges of the bench, with your thumbs facing forwards and your fingers gripping the under-edge of the bench. This will give you good leverage

- Then adopt the same method of kicking to handstand as described on page 41. If you perform the movement with confidence you will find that gripping the bench helps you to create the necessary force and to control your balance much more efficiently.

TEACHING TIPS

- Be aware that gymnasts are likely to topple over, so teach them how to turn out of the movement by moving one of their hands forwards and cartwheeling down on to the floor.

- Place additional matting where they may fall.

- This is not a suitable movement for the gymnast who is not competent in rescuing an overbalance situation, as the height of the bench makes it quite difficult to roll.

Handstand on a bench.

HANGING AND SWINGING

The swing and hang family of gymnastics skills involves more advanced apparatus, including the high or low bar, parallel bars and rings. Of these, the most challenging are the rings, because of their unstable nature.

UPSTART ON LOW BAR

The upstart basically allows the gymnast to move from a position of hang to a position of support, or from a position below the bar to a position above the bar. The upstart movement on the low bar, parallel bars and rings is very similar, but a slightly different technique is required in each case.

On a low bar:

- Stand facing the apparatus with the bar at shoulder height.

- Jumping upwards off the ground and simultaneously reaching forward to grasp the bar, pike slightly at the waist to allow your body to swing with your hands in overgrasp and your legs stretched out in front.

 Upstart on low bar.

- When your body is as far forwards as possible it is extended into a straight line with the shoulders pressing back against the bar.

- As the return swing begins, bend rapidly at the waist, bringing your feet in close to the bar.

- As your body swings back under the bar, drive back forcefully with your legs to the straight line position, at the same time pressing down on the bar with your hands and arms.

- Then push the bar along the body, from the ankle to the thigh, without making contact with your legs. The upstart is completed as your body continues to rotate up into front support.

TEACHING TIP

The hands must be moved around the bar in advance of the body's rotation to allow for a strong front support position to be achieved. A common fault with all beginners is that they rotate around the wrist and not around the bar, so they arrive on top of the apparatus with their hands forced backwards into a position that prevents them from supporting themselves properly. It is important to note that in the case of most bar skills it is normal for the fingers to be trailing around the bar, but in the upstart, the body works against the fingers so the hands have to be shifted very quickly to the required position.

Francesca Vincent performs the upstart on a low bar.

CAST/BEAT TO HANDSTAND ON LOW BAR

- Starting from the front support position, with the bar at thigh level and your hands in either the overgrasp or undergrasp position, bend forwards.

- Move the bar position from thigh to waist.

- Swing your legs forwards at the same time as you bend forwards, then drive your legs quickly and forcefully backwards while pressing down on the bar with your hands.

- Keep your shoulders low as your legs swing to an inverted position above the bar.

- Your body will need to be tense when it is straight in order to transfer the swing from the legs to the rest of the body.

- This straightening of the body will cause the body to rise upwards towards the handstand position and the arms can be locked straight.

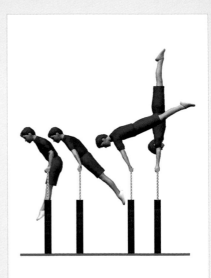

Cast/beat to handstand on low bar.

The beat to handstand requires a delicate combination of swing and strength.

DISMOUNTING

It is extremely important that once beginner gymnasts start to achieve the handstand, they are able to dismount both ways from the bar, either by falling forwards or backwards from handstand. It is essential that gymnasts learn this particular skill on a low bar, so they are aware of the various options available.

Practice on the floor

Practise handstand push-ups on the floor to improve shoulder strength. Try not to hollow your back.

PARALLEL BARS

Nearly all work done on parallel bars is part of the 'swing' family of gymnastics. Exercises on parallel bars must consist of swing, flight and field elements, and may also contain a certain amount of strength work.

Due to the nature of the apparatus, special attention must be given to the development of swing and support strength. For young gymnasts, special adaptation kits may be needed to reduce the distance between the two bars. The bars should be roughly shoulder-width apart. A good measurement is the distance between the elbow and the hand. If a gymnast is able to touch the bars with their elbows and fingertips, then the bars are at a suitable width.

SWINGING ON PARALLEL BARS

- The swing is a pendulum movement in which your shoulders first move forwards and your feet backwards.

- Your shoulders then move backwards as your feet swing forwards. This is to keep your balance on top of the bars.

- Swing from the chest and shoulders, with a slight kick of your feet at the bottom of the forward swing.

- Hold the body straight.

▼ A gymnast swinging on parallel bars. The shoulders move in the opposite direction to the feet to maintain balance.

▲ Upstart on parallel bars.

UPSTART ON PARALLEL BARS

- Swing forwards in hang maintaining complete extension in the shoulders. Your feet will glide forwards just above the bars due to a slight flexing at the hips.

- As you reach this fully extended position, quickly bend at the hips and bring your feet to your hands.

- Swing back in this position, bringing your legs close to your face.

- As your shoulders begin to rise on the return swing, extend your hips forcefully and perform a strong downward push through straight arms to raise the body to front support.

- The upward thrust is therefore created during this latter part of the swing, which is a backward and upward pendulum movement.

▲ Practising the swing to handstand with two benches allows the gymnast to develop the required skills before attempting them on the bars.

SWING TO HANDSTAND ON PARALLEL BARS

This skill should first be practised by kicking to handstand on the floor, using two chalk lines drawn on the floor to indicate the bars. The lines should be drawn shoulder-width apart.

Having successfully mastered the handstand on the two chalk lines without moving your hands, you can transfer to two benches, starting with the benches side by side:

- Kick to handstand from the benches.

- Slowly widen the gap between the two benches until it is equivalent to the width of the performer's shoulders.

To transfer this skill to the low parallel bars, start on the end of the bars facing outwards. Kick to handstand and then finally attempt the swing to handstand.

- If you fail to make the handstand, move your shoulders forwards to control the return from the swing. Failure to do this could risk the arms collapsing.

- If you kick or swing too hard, you can turn out of the movement into a quarter-turn, or drop over on to the safety mat that has been placed at the end of the bars.

- Once you have mastered the swing to handstand successfully on the end of the bars, you will be able to transfer it to the middle. Take extra care if you topple over, as you must push strongly from one arm to come down on one side of the bars.

TEACHING TIP

Support this skill in the first instance by holding the gymnast's shoulder with one hand whilst lifting the hips with the other.

▼ Swing to handstand on parallel bars.

SWINGING ON THE RINGS

The rings offer a unique challenge to the gymnast because of their instability.

- Keeping your hips and shoulders tight, initiate the swing from your shoulders. Keep your arms straight.
- At the end of each swing, push the rings away from you and slightly apart.
- Maintain pressure on the rings at all times.
- Your body should rise upwards in the swing due to its pendulum motion and to the downward pressure of the hands.

UPSTART ON THE RINGS

The upstart is one of the basic methods of getting above the rings and of moving from hanging to a position of support.

- Start from an inverted hang, with your feet above your head and your hands at the side of your body.
- Pike your body deeply with your knees, dropping very close to your face without pause. Then extend your feet forcefully to the ceiling in an upward and forward direction whilst simultaneously pressing down on the rings towards your hips. This will bring your shoulders up above the rings.

Swinging on the rings.

TEACHING TIP

The rings must be kept close to the body to maintain control. Once the legs have been forcefully extended away, the key to this skill is to flex quickly at the hips and maintain a piked position during the upward and forward movement of the body. This movement is created through alternate flexing and contracting of the legs and trunk.

Upstart on the rings.

HANDSTAND ON THE RINGS

The handstand is more difficult to perform on the rings than on the floor or parallel bars because of the unsteady nature of the rings.

- The handstand should be held without the arms or body touching the wires. Control should emanate through the wrist and not through the shoulder.

- To achieve the correct position, the rings should be turned slightly outwards, with the gymnast's thumbs turned away from one another. This will help bring the arms into a straight position.

TEACHING TIPS

- The handstand is best practised on 'lower' rings, for example kicking up from a low box or pressing up into the position from a raised platform.

- Two people should help to stabilise the rings by pulling down on them on both sides while the gymnast learns to balance on them.

- It is important that the gymnast is able to control the handstand successfully on the floor before attempting this skill on either the parallel bars or rings.

◀ Displacement of the rings.

▼ Handstand on the rings.

BEAM WORK

In principle, the exercises performed on the beam are technically the same as those performed on the floor, with slight variations induced by the narrowness (10cm) of the apparatus.

ENGLAND

▲ England's Beth Tweddle competes on the beam during the Commonwealth Games, Manchester 2002.

STARTING BEAM WORK

To gain confidence on the beam, start by practising the skills on a low bench before transferring them to a low beam. Some of the more difficult moves should be practised with a mat over the beam.

One of the most important aspects of beam work is posture, and from the very beginning composure and control are essential.

General practice should include the following:

- Walking briskly along the beam keeping hips and shoulders in line.

- Jumps, jetés, split jumps.

- Turns. All turns and pivots should be performed on the toes. As you turn, raise your arms above your head and rise up on to your toes.

- Turns on two feet. Standing with one foot in front of the other, extend your legs and ankles until you are on your toes. At the same time, swing your arms up and slightly to one side, creating a twist at the shoulders. Push through the front leg and perform a half-turn, taking the weight evenly on both feet.

TEACHING TIP

Beginners have a tendency to lose their balance as their feet squat to the beam. Support them under their shoulders so they have good control.

SQUAT-ON MOUNT

- Face the beam.
- Place your hands on the beam, shoulder-width apart.
- Jump from both feet and press down with the hands.
- As your hips rise, squat your feet between your hands.
- Transfer your weight to your feet and stand up.

Squat-on mount on to the beam.

STRADDLE MOUNT FROM FRONT SUPPORT

- Place your hands on the beam with your fingers just over and gripping the far edge
- Jump to front support.
- Push on one hand and swing the leg of the same side over the beam. Simultaneously transfer your weight to the other hand.
- As your leg rises above the height of the beam and begins to swing forwards over the beam,

momentarily raise your free hand to allow it to pass over the apparatus.

- On replacing the hand, quarter-turn the body to face the supporting hand and sit astride the beam.
- Place both hands in front of you and press down, allowing your shoulders to move forwards. As your legs swing backwards, bring them up to squat on to the beam.

Straddle mount from front support.

HALF-SPIN ON ONE FOOT

- Step forwards on to an extended leg and foot.

- Raise your arms above your head to initiate the turn.

- Hold your head up. When you have completed the turn, fix your gaze back on the end of the beam.

- You can turn inwards or outwards. The inward turn is normally easier.

Half-spin on one foot.

FORWARD ROLL ON BEAM

Practise this skill on a bench at first.

- Your thumbs should be along the beam, your hands down the side.

- The roll should be performed fairly quickly but with good control.

- Finish the roll as you would on the floor, but place one foot slightly in front of the other.

- Reach well forwards with your arms, and when your weight is on your feet stand up.

Forward roll.

TEACHING TIP

Placing a mat on the beam and taking hold of the gymnast's hand or arm as they attempt to stand up will greatly help them with the forward roll on beam.

Cartwheel.

CARTWHEEL ON BEAM

Practise this on a line on the floor, and ask your coach to check that each hand and foot makes contact with the line.

- The cartwheel on the beam is the same as a cartwheel performed on the floor except the head and eyes watch the beam all the way through the movement.

- The second foot is placed closer to, and facing, the hands. For better grip, the foot can be placed slightly at an angle across the beam so the toes can grip the edge of the apparatus.

HANDSTAND ON BEAM

This movement should be performed initially on the floor or on a floor beam.

- The handstand can be performed with the legs straight, split, or with one leg bent and one leg straight (this is called the 'stag' position).

- The technique is exactly the same as when performed on the floor except the thumbs are placed along the beam and the fingers down the side of the beam.

- The back leg is kept straight. The arms are raised above the head in the early stages.

TEACHING TIP

If gymnasts have difficulty placing their feet back on to the beam after the support on hands, position yourself so that you can support them in this second phase of the cartwheel. If the beam is too high, stand on a box top or platform.

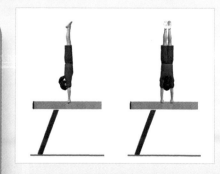

Handstand on beam.

GYMNASTICS CHRONOLOGY

2000 BC Gymnastic activities are depicted on Egyptian artefacts.

800 BC Gymnastics becomes popular in ancient Greece and gymnasias (marked courtyards) are used for running, jumping and wrestling.

510 BC The ascendence of the Roman Empire means gymnastics takes a back seat to military training. The wooden horse is introduced.

AD 393 Emperor Theodosius abolishes the ancient Olympic Games and gymnastics declines and is all but forgotten for centuries.

Late 1700s Johann Friedrich GutsMuths (1759–1839) designs a programme of exercises to improve balance and suppleness as well as muscular strength. His follower, Friedrich Ludwig Jahn (1778–1852), develops early models of the beam, horizontal bar, parallel bars and the vault.

1804 The Crown Prince of Denmark believes gymnastics to be useful for military training and creates the Military Gymnastic Institute in 1804.

1860 The German Gymnastics Club, the first civilian federation, is formed.

1881 The European Federation of Gymnastics (FEG) is founded on 23 July in Liège, Belgium, making it the oldest international sporting organisation. There are three members: Belgium, France and the Netherlands.

1896 Men's gymnastics is included in the first Modern Olympic Games in Athens, Greece. It includes events such as rope-climbing and club-swinging.

1903 The first World Artistic Gymnastics Championships are held in Antwerp, Belgium. France tops the medal table with two golds and one silver.

1921 The FEG admits the first non-European countries and the organisation is re-named Fédération Internationale de Gymnastique (FIG) on 7 April.

1928 The first women's Olympic competition (synchronised callisthenics) is held in Amsterdam.

1953 The first World Gymnaestrada (the largest general gymnastics exhibition) is held in Rotterdam, Netherlands. Held every four years, thousands of participants of all ages perform in huge group performances.

1954 Olympic Games apparatus, events and the scoring system (1–10) for both men and women are standardised in the modern format.

1961 The Fédération Internationale de Gymnastique (FIG) recognise rhythmic gymnastics as a discipline.

1963 The first World Rhythmic Gymnastics Championships are held in Budapest, Hungary. Ten countries take part, and the Soviet Union tops the medal table with a total of seven medals.

1964 The first Trampolining World Championships are held in London, UK.

1965 The International Trampolining Federation is formed in Twickenham, UK.

1976 At the age of 14, Nadia Comaneci of Romania becomes one of the stars at the Olympic Games in Montreal, Canada when she receives the first perfect score.

1984 Rhythmic gymnastics is introduced as an Olympic sport in Los Angeles, USA.

1995 Fédération Internationale de Gymnastique (FIG) holds its first World Aerobics Championships.

1996 Fédération Internationale de Gymnastique (FIG) adopts sport aerobics as a gymnastics discipline.

1999 The International Trampolining Federation becomes part of the Fédération Internationale de Gymnastique (FIG).

2000 Individual trampoline is included in the Olympic Games, Sydney, Australia, as an additional gymnastic sport.

2001 The traditional vaulting horse is replaced with a new apparatus, known as a tongue or table, which is ultimately more stable and therefore safer.

2006 A new points system is introduced to decrease the chance of gymnasts receiving a perfect score. Instead, the gymnast's start value depends on the difficulty rating of the exercise routine. The deductions are also higher.

2008 Louis Smith is the first British Individual gymnastics medallist in a century, at the 2008 Beijing Olympics, claiming Bronze in the pommel horse final.

GLOSSARY

Apparatus The equipment used in gymnastics.

Approach run In the adult competition, part one of four in the vault, consisting of a 25m run to the trampette to mount the vault in the adult competition.

Arabesque A pose on one leg. The other leg extends behind the body, which lowers from the hips to form a curve.

Astride With a leg on each side, or legs wide apart.

Balance beam In the adult competition, a 5m beam, 10cm wide and 1.2m above the floor. Gymnasts perform routines on the beam including twists, leaps and tumbles.

Balance position A static position, holding a distinct shape.

Cardiorespiratory system Consists of the lungs, heart, blood vessels and the blood, and is responsible for the uptake and transport of oxygen throughout the body and for the disposal of waste.

Cardiovascular system Sometimes called the circulatory system, it consists of the heart, arteries, veins and capillaries. The heart pumps the blood through the various vessels in a circulatory fashion.

Dismount To leave an apparatus at the end of a routine.

Equilateral triangle A triangle in which all three sides have equal length.

Handspring A spring off the hands. The hands are placed on the floor and there is a strong push from the shoulders to spring up.

Hurdle step From a short run the gymnast hops over a low barrier to land on two feet.

Inverted hang Hanging upside down with a straight body, usually performed on the rings.

Jeté A move where the gymnast springs from one foot to the other.

Landing Part four of four parts in the vault, where the gymnast resumes a standing position after the post-flight phase (see post-flight), landing on two feet on the floor. The landing also describes the dismount from all apparatus and the final phase of a tumble.

Muscular-skeletal system Consists of muscles, tendons and ligaments and the skeleton, which, in combination, support and protect vital organs and body structures and also allow movement of the body.

Neuromuscular system Consists of the nervous system and the muscles, which work together to permit movement of the body.

Overgrasp Swinging on the bar with the palm of the hand and fingers facing away from the gymnast.

Pike Body position where the body is bent forward 90 degrees at the waist with the legs kept straight.

Pivot A turn on the ball of the foot.

Post-flight Part three of four in the vault, consisting of the time from the gymnast's hands hitting the vault to returning to an upright position. Advanced competitors may perform one or more twists and somersaults in this phase.

Pre-flight Part two of four in the vault, consisting of the time after the gymnast's feet have hit the springboard and before the gymnast's hands hit the vaulting horse.

Quarter-turn When a gymnast turns 90 degrees, either on the floor or in the air.

Routine A combination of moves and sequences performed on one apparatus.

Split jumps A leap from one foot, making a 'splits' position in the air and landing on the opposite foot.

Spotting Spotting a landing place before taking off.

Springboard A platform set upon multiple springs, which allows the gymnast greater propulsion when jumped on.

Supporting When a second person assists the gymnast through a move, and prepares to cushion them to avoid injury in the event of a fall.

Tuck A position where the knees are bent into the chest, with the body folded at the waist.

Walkover A move where a gymnast transfers from a standing position to a handstand to a standing position once again.

INDEX

THE DYBBUK

Dedicated to the memory of
Rabbi Hugo Gryn